ISBN 0-7683-2059-3

Library of Congress Catalog Card Number 98-43022

Text by Flavia and Lisa Weedn
Illustrations by Flavia Weedn
© Weedn Family Trust
www.flavia.com
All rights reserved

Published in 1999 by Cedco Publishing Company
100 Pelican Way, San Rafael, California 94901
For a free catalog of other Cedco® products, please write
to the address above, or visit our website: www.cedco.com

Printed in China

The artwork for each picture is digitally mastered using acrylic on canvas.

With love and gratitude to those kindred spirits whose
dedication, endless support, and talented hands made this book
a reality — Lisa Mansfield, Jane Durand, Diana Musacchio, Tyler
Tomblin, Jennie Sparrow, Solveig Chandler, Kim Gendreau,
Annette Berlin, Hui-Ying Ting-Bornfreund.

If I could sit across the porch from God,

I'd thank Him for the glory of

the morning, and for starry skies.

I'd thank Him for the magic of a

child's soft smile, for memories, and

for this wonderful feeling we call

love. I'd thank Him for the hopes

and dreams of this sweet life, but

most of all, I'd thank Him for

lending me you.

Across the Porch from God

Flavia and Lisa Weedn

Illustrated by Flavia Weedn

Cedco Publishing Company • San Rafael, California

Authors' Note

This book is the blending of two generations, that of mother and daughter. Side by side, we offer a deeply personal view into the window of our lives, for each story written is a true account of hope and challenge, faith and vision. Our words are simple, uncluttered, and speak solely from the heart. Our greatest wish is that within the authenticity of our storytelling, you will find a resonating corner, a common thread of understanding, and a reason to believe.

TABLE OF CONTENTS

In every ordinary day there are a thousand

miracles, if only we have eyes to see them.

We all share in the sweet mystery of life.

We love, feel, cry, care and believe. We yearn

to become more and to help others, as we

strive to make a difference, however grand or small.

Deep inside every one of us, there exists a source of belief,

a light encouraging us onward.

However we choose to describe it, faith is the

expression of hope. It is the sound of comfort,

the recognition of beauty, the healing touch that moves

us forward. Yet there are times when we may be so

busy looking ahead that we forget to look up,

and the light within us may be difficult to see.

When life's simplistic beauty eludes us, we need only

open the window, throw open the curtains, and view

the rich landscape of our ordinary moments as reverently

as our divine ones, to bring the wonder back into view.

This slight change in perspective can dramatically

transform us. In this book, we have shared our personal

experiences and our own private conversations with God.

Some are quite ordinary, others divinely extraordinary,

but each made a difference in our lives.

We hope this view into our world will remind you of the

simple wonders that are a part of yours, and that

you will take time to pause and feel the gratitude

for the many blessings which surround you.

Flavia

Life's moments

are woven into

songs

and silences

only the heart

can hear.

Sacred Moments

That which the heart has cherished becomes a part of us forever.

Music for the Soul

by Flavia Weedn

The windows of our lives reflect that which is important to us, that which we value most, and that which is sacred to the heart. The moments we cherish are not all part of the grand and the great, often they are pieces of the ordinary — beautiful times in which we have found joy, comfort, and love.

Unlike major events in our lives, there are no photos nor writings to describe them. These simple stories, recorded by the heart, define our values, reflect our virtues, and tell us who we are. Combined, they give us a sense of self. They are the stuff we are made of. A particular sight or sound can quickly allow us to re-live one of these moments. It is wondrous when this happens, for it brings to our minds a state of grace.

A stack of old china plates lay on a table at a garage sale. The sight of a familiar pattern on one of them instantly took me back to my grandmother's kitchen to a time long ago. I was seven years old. My grandmother and I had just finished washing her dishes, patterned like these. I was standing on a chair, trying to reach the middle shelf of her cupboard to put the plates away when one slipped from my hand. She caught it in midair.

What I remember most is not the pounding of my heart, but my grandmother's gentle smile when she looked up at me, and said tenderly, "Don't worry, honey, it's only a plate." In that very moment, I knew again how much she loved me.

A small piece of time sparked by the sight of a dinner plate — unimportant to many, but a magical moment to a seven-year-old, and one my heart had chosen to keep.

༄

I sat rocking my baby daughter for what seemed to be endless hours. She was very ill, and I, tired and deeply concerned, had gone without sleep for two nights. Suddenly I heard the sound of my mother's car in the driveway, and was filled with an instant relief. I heard her car door close, and the feeling of knowing she was near surrounded me with the same warm comfort she always brought to me when I was in need. I felt blessed.

Just the sound of a car and its door closing — but simple moments that mattered greatly, for there is a unique kind of magic in knowing someone you love is near.

༄

I was alone in San Francisco for a short while, working with a master printer. On my way back to my hotel one evening, someone grabbed my purse from my shoulder, and disappeared around the corner. It was dark by the time I returned to my empty hotel room. Nervous about the way my artwork was turning out, and still upset over being robbed, I pulled a chair up close to the window. I found some leftover bread and cheese, used the windowsill as a table, and began to eat my dinner. Staring at the world outside, I felt very alone.

Out of the darkness, suddenly neon lights spelling out *Ballroom* began to blink, then to glow from the hotel across the street. Faint musical sounds of a 1940's band floated through my window. A line up of old cars and cabs pulled in front of the lobby, and elderly men all dressed in white escorted elderly women, all dressed in white, into the lobby and up to the third floor ballroom.

I could see clearly into the large ballroom window, and watched white gloves, corsages and three-piece suits slow dance on the dance floor. As the night wore on, the music filled my room, and prisms of light from the luminous chandelier danced like fireflies in the darkness. Caught up in the wonder of the music and the romance for life I felt within me, my loneliness disappeared.

From my window, I knew I was viewing some kind of elegant affair, to which, in some unexplained way, I had been invited. This made me feel part of the beauty of the night, and I looked down at the meager meal on the windowsill and smiled to myself. I got up and started dancing. Not in that ballroom, but in my hotel room. And not alone, for I, barefoot and in my robe, began dancing with the memory of another moment in time — one my heart had saved.

I celebrate the magic of that night and other experiences like it. To me, they are all part of the wonder of life, and lead me forward on my journey to becoming who I am.

I was painting professionally at home while my children were still young. For years I used the same old Mason jar where I rinsed my brushes. In order to remove excess water after rinsing them, I had a habit of tapping the side of each brush several times on the top inside rim of the jar. During the holidays, I would re-paint or re-create ordinary objects, transform them into new art forms, and give them as gifts. One such object was this paint-stained Mason jar.

I took my oldest brushes, some with bristles worn down to the metal, and attached them securely to the inside of the jar. By adding coats of varnish, it became a permanent sculpture, and was the gift I gave to my son that Christmas.

On a recent visit to his home, I noticed this sculpture still standing on his nightstand. I asked him why he had kept it in such a visible place after such a long time, and not hidden in a corner or packed away somewhere. He told me it was because each time he looked at the jar, he thought of me. He could still hear the sound made years ago when he was young, as I tapped the brushes against the glass rim. It made him remember times when he would wake up frightened late at night and always be consoled when he heard that sound. To him it meant I was very close, just in the next room painting — and he would go back to sleep, knowing that everything was going to be alright. He said that sound would always be magic to him.

My gratitude grew at the thought of this, for I have tried to gift my children with some of the wonder I have found in being alive. One of the joys I feel is seeing the way their hearts look at life and how they, as adults, have managed to keep the magic that all children are born with. Never ignoring it as they grew up, never letting the world take it away, they have held onto it as a light of hope, and kept it alive.

We can all see and embrace the beauty and love in this world, if we listen to the moments of magic cherished by our hearts. They are the music that touches our souls.

*The human spirit
needs a private place
to dwell — a sanctuary
where passions come
alive and dreams are
made visible.*

Peace in the Garden

by Lisa Weedn

It is an hour before dawn and the house is whisper quiet. I make a pot of coffee and step into my studio. A favorite movie poster, hanging center stage on the wall, catches my eye, as if to greet me. It announces *A Room with a View* in full-color Italian bliss. "Yes," I think to myself, "this is a room with a view. We all have our place. This is mine."

I have seen much from this room. It is my sanctuary, my peace, my island of creation. I write, think, and dream here. I've fallen in love in this room. Here I've known hurt and the grace of healing. I've talked to God and learned about life within these vivid walls.

The morning is cool and I cradle the warmth of my coffee cup. I breathe in the vision of my crowded bookshelves, perusing cherished volumes that speak the wisdom of the world. They seem to smile back at me, as if they can hear my thoughts, taste my gratitude.

Scraps of fabric, saved pieces of broken china, old buttons and glass mosaic chips fill jars next to my easel. Paintbrushes stained with rainbowed streaks occupy ceramic pitchers and cobalt blue vases. Half-finished canvases and poems hungering for their final lines lie in wait. "This is my garden," I say to myself. Here is where I plant the delicate seeds of my soul and nurture them until they bloom. Some thrive, others still need tending. But patiently they await my touch, just as I await theirs.

I sit at my desk and sigh at the stacks of paper, the cluttered display of my passion. I turn to the starkness of a page that beckons my attention. Just one more story to compose and the chapter will be complete. I think upon the message I yearn to deliver. It is perhaps the simplest message of all, and yet the most important. What tale will tell it best? What memory can I draw from? What seeds can I sow upon this paper that others might reap? The moment feels fertile, important somehow.

I hum a familiar tune as I think about life — the reach of God's touch, of people and love and nature, of beauties so rich they have no words. I stop to wonder how many others feel as passionately as I do this morning, filled with the miracle of just being alive and a part of it all. Whether they travel the globe, feed the hungry, sell flowers on a street corner, or just sip coffee nestled in their own little place in the world, I trust in my heart that I am not alone. In spite of the different paths we follow, we are all connected in the

great mystery of life. This is the gift we share. This is what I thank God for. This is what I need to write. My hands begin their dance.

The first ray of light appears through my window and I know my private hour is coming to a pause. Soon there will be a meal to make, a school lunch to pack, a child's hair to braid and books to gather. I write one last line, here in my room with a view, and breathe in the vision of my paradise so that I may carry it with me until I return. Then I rise to go wake my daughter.

I walk down the hall and hear the faint sound of a child humming. I enter the kitchen to find her perched at the counter, painting a picture. For a brief moment she doesn't hear me, and so I watch. As her hands dance across the paper, I realize that she, too, has found her place, her peaceful sanctuary. At six years old, she already shares the gift.

Finally, she looks up at me, her sky blue eyes gleaming in the morning light, and says, "Look, Mama. I made it for you. Do you like my garden?"

We are

unaware

of what

sweet miracles

may come.

The Locket

by Flavia Weedn

$\mathcal{I}$t is no secret that I believe life is filled with wonder. I've never known if this belief is based upon the fact that life has brought me wonderful moments, or if the moments happened because I believed that life would bring them to me — but come they do.

We were driving along the coast on our way home. The rain had finally stopped. I was looking up, drinking in the magnificence of the sky — its clarity, the brilliance of its blue, and the billowing whiteness of the huge, low moving clouds. Suddenly I became acutely aware of the incredible beauty of this world, and how we take it all for granted until something happens to remind us. In a silent moment I gave thanks to God for the gifts of this sweet life.

On an impulse, we turned inland on a small, slightly winding road surrounded by tall, fragrant eucalyptus trees and hillsides the color of green seen only following a rain. After some twenty miles off of the main road, we came upon a very small town. On the main street, there was a service station, a diner, a boarded-up motel, and a truck junkyard. There were

no sidewalks on which to walk, only wooden planks or dirt paths. We saw no one on the streets, and the town was so quiet, it beckoned to be discovered.

While my son was buying gasoline, I looked for a church whose bell tower I had seen from the road. I discovered instead a small, but beautiful Spanish mission over two hundred years old. Its voice was in the faded colors of the cracked paint still visible on its doors and windows. It spoke of times past, of warmth, love and care for the people that had lived in this town. Weathered by years, it stood tall and proud with flowering vines and wildflowers encircling, almost protecting it. Large terracotta pots, smoothed by the wind of age, were still overflowing with bright orange, yellow and purple blossoms. Its stone fence framed a small cemetery where shade from the huge oak trees created shadow patterns on the gravestones and the blue ground cover that bloomed around them. Everything around it was so still, as though forgotten by time. Unlike anything I had ever seen before, I was spellbound by the beauty and the wonder I had stumbled upon.

My son joined me and as we walked back toward the car, he smiled and pointed to an old sign hanging from a post which read: *Antique Shop*. He knew how much I enjoyed browsing in shops like these when I could steal the time. We decided to take the time, so he,

who felt the same way about truck junkyards, walked in one direction, and I in the other.

The shop was the rear room of an old frame house. Partially hidden by trees, it was on a street that looked like a facade from an old movie set. I marveled how anyone could stay in business there. When I saw the *For Sale* sign, I realized that perhaps one couldn't.

The yard had large handcarved wooden angel sculptures, handmade wind chimes; patina bells hanging from ropes, and old high chairs covered with lush grapevines. Three bathtubs filled with flourishing water lilies were surrounded by a garden of blooms. In the middle of this forgotten, dusty town, flowers were growing abundantly around this house. Smiling, I thought to myself, if it were this garden that was for sale, I'd buy it.

The proprietor, a woman who obviously owned the house and shop, greeted me graciously. When I asked how it was that her garden could thrive so well in all the heat and dust that was everywhere around her, her answer surprised me. She said she had discovered a river two miles from her house that, from underground, fed anything she planted. "Like a miracle," she told me.

Entering the room, I quietly looked around until my eyes fell upon a small doll. Immediately a strange feeling of familiarity came over me. In some odd way,

I felt I had not only seen her face before, but had held and loved it. She was very old, her arms and legs were jointed, and with the exception of a few scrapes, everything including her clothing was original. She was beautiful.

I explained my feelings to the proprietor, who told me the doll was from the late 1930's, and agreed its face seemed unusual for a doll. I came to the conclusion I must have had a doll like this as a child, which would explain everything. I asked her the price, and she said, without hesitation, "It doesn't matter, I want you to have it. The doll belongs to you . . . it's yours." More than astonished, I insisted I pay whatever the price, but she wouldn't accept any money. I could see that for some reason, it was very important to her that she give me this doll.

"Thank you so much, but please tell me why," I asked again. "Because I know you'll love it," she said.

I started to leave when I noticed a piece of jewelry caught in the shine of the sun as it reflected off a glass case in the corner of the room. It was a small, gold locket with an inlay of crescent moon and stars made of tiny diamond chips. I was in a state of disbelief, for it was a child's version and exact replica of a 1920's locket my daughter gave to me years ago. The very one Sylvie, my adored six-year-old granddaughter, loves and wears each time she visits me. The one we've had

many conversations about, and the one I promised would be hers one day.

When my son met me, he recognized the locket, and was as overwhelmed as I that I had found it. When I showed him the doll, he said, "Mama, look closely at her face, don't you recognize the doll?" And then with a wonderful expression, said, "It looks just like Sylvie."

Whether it's the discovery of an underground river that keeps flowers growing in a distant, lonesome town, a great kindness from a stranger, the face of a doll, or a small gold locket, it's the same. Small joys and blessings like this often come to us when we're not looking and least expecting them.

Small miracles they're called, many of which we can never explain. I believe that each is a precious and golden moment God gives to us — one to be cherished and to remind us of the love, wonder and surprises that wait for us all through our lives.

*A*ngels are

all around us,

and any H E A R T

who *yearns* to

can reach out

and touch a wing.

In the Company of Angels

*It is the wise
and shining spirits
in this life who
find love in
small things, and
are richly blessed.*

An Air of Joy

by Flavia Weedn

My mother was genteel. God gave her grace and a classic inner beauty. She was feminine and had a tender strength. She held love in her pocket and gave it freely to everyone she ever met.

Her background was Southern. She was born not of money, prestige or finery, but of giving and gracious hearts. She loved life with a passion and had a unique way of embracing every moment as a miracle. She never forgot to thank God for small blessings, for she knew that in small things there existed great virtues. To this day, she remains the richest woman I have ever known.

Love and family were the most important things to my mother. They were always what mattered in her life. She instilled in us a deep appreciation for one another, for all people and for God. She had a shining spirit and no matter where she was, whenever she entered a room, she brought light.

When my brother, sister and I were nearly grown, my mother began working part-time for our dentist, Dr. Whitney. He hired her as a temporary office manager, but she worked there for years and became much more. She had a unique gift of making others feel confident, important and appreciated. Her presence, her touch, created an air of joy.

Dr. Whitney came from a very different kind of background; one of education, wealth, and social status. He was single, lived in an estate with a name, had servants, security systems, and iron gates. He was years younger than my mother and the one who gave her the nickname, *Gramma*. Soon everyone in his office building called her *Gramma*, and they'd often say that since she had begun working there, Dr. Whitney seemed a different person. In many ways, Dr. Whitney had the same effect on her. We could see it in my mother's eyes and hear it in her voice.

As time passed, Dr. Whitney became like family. We attended his elegant dinner parties, and he spent summer afternoons eating ripe apricots on our back porch. At his home, my mother met movie stars and other celebrities, and she was so at ease with herself and with them, they would often become friends before she even knew who they were.

Dr. Whitney's holiday celebrations were large and glamorous events. His Christmas Eve gatherings were spectacular, and they were my mother's favorites. This season was a time my mother's spirit absolutely danced. Giving was what she did most and, so true to her nature, she was unaware that she was giving at all. She had a natural eye for design, and brought the look and feel and true spirit of the holidays into our home, as well as into his. If she could, she would have decorated the world and cradled it in her love. If everyone in the world had known her, they would have loved her back.

My mother's Christmas presents to Dr. Whitney were well thought out and always something she had spent long hours pouring her heart into. His presents to her were extravagant and expensive, yet simple and fitting. The closer it got to Christmas, the more my mother's anticipation grew like that of a child's, for she knew his presents were going to be different from anything else she had ever received. He knew how to reach her soul. He would give her perfume, hand carried from Paris, with a name that would move her to tears; or a necklace with a shimmering golden angel sitting on top of the world. At the angel's feet, there would be a small engraving of my mother's name.

Every year when he vacationed, Dr. Whitney sent her postcards and letters describing in great detail where he went and the beauty he witnessed. My mother had never traveled, but she saw the world through his eyes. She kept every photo and saved every word he ever wrote in a See's candy box under her bed.

He brought her operas, she gave him biscuits and gravy. He talked about world affairs, she wondered the color of the wind. He gave her tulips from Holland for her garden, she gave him geraniums from cuttings for his. He took her for rides in his Porsche, and she taught him Southern folk songs. They were from different times, with different life experiences, but each gave the other such needed and cherished gifts. They were fortunate enough to have found a way to give what they each had to give. Together they found the joy in true friendship, and together they celebrated being alive.

My mother's spirit sang the song she believed in. She was authentic and true, and it was from her that I learned how to find beauty in the ordinary. It was from her we all learned that giving love is life's greatest gift. She treated us, her children, as if we were her finest and most sacred treasures — and she did so uncritically and unconditionally. She owned this kind of love.

When she prayed, she talked with God as though He were sitting in a chair in our living room. She revered Him and we grew up knowing that He held us in His hands and loved us with all of His heart. If she thought the world was about to end, my mother would

still have watered her geraniums. And if she couldn't, she believed there would always be someone who would. She owned this kind of faith.

My mother gave me childhood memories of how she loved the mornings. With a cup of coffee in her hand, she would stand at the window, look up at the sky and tell me she felt certain that something very wonderful was going to happen that day. Whether or not it ever happened didn't matter. She always believed it would. And so did I.

I think of her daily, and I thank God she was my mother. I am so grateful for the love she showed me, for the memories she gave, and for the blessings that were born during the time we shared together. I still own them. I always will. Love is the beauty we take with us wherever we go.

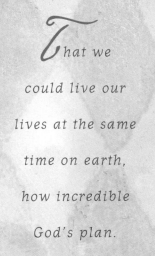

*That we
could live our
lives at the same
time on earth,
how incredible
God's plan.*

Forever

by Lisa Weedn

We sat at a corner cafe, sipping a warm, sweet brew against the backdrop of a bustling city's night parade. Two souls captured by the grace of the moment, oblivious to the motioning motion surrounding us. Oblivious to time, and to our otherwise distanced lives. Our eyes fixed on one another's reflection, we drank in the blessing, the music shared between us, the miracle of this night. We quenched our thirst by composing silent lyrics only our hearts could hear, for we knew all too well this moment would have to keep us. It would have to last.

"*He* planned this, you know," said my friend with the wise eyes of a holy man. "Do you understand?" he continued, his voice softening to a hush.

"Yes," I whispered, smiling, taking his hand in mine. "I have many questions for God, but concerning you I can only offer praise. It's heaven just to know you exist."

Then, like so many times before, my smile melted into tears. Tears of joy. Tears of gratitude. Tears spilling under an antique moon, revealing the ache that soon, too soon, we'd have to say goodbye. Again.

37

We first met three years before. A chance meeting at a writer's forum proved to be our fate. He wrote truths that caused my very foundation to tremble. His words were the same as those I had only heard my inner voice speak in solitude — visions and private conversations I thought were reserved for me and me alone. Was he an angel sent to greet me? A messenger of some all-important truth? All I knew was that his presence assured me I was not alone, nor would I ever be. I had found a soul companion, my twin, and here he was breathing life into me. I was, and continue to be, in awe of the blessing.

Through common dreams and soulful prose, we've shared lifetimes in these few precious years. Despite the miles that separate us, we've become pieces of one another. Once single threads, we are now woven into a cable so strong that nothing can ever break or tear its beauty. Never have I been so certain of anything, or anyone. Herein is faith.

I have no name for what this relationship is. Surely others have wondered, and some have asked. I can only say that this is a kinship deeper than I ever dreamt possible — the kind that makes me happy to be alive. We share a taste of heaven, he and I, and my only wish is that every soul on earth might know this glory.

Much of what he brings me is too big, too profound for words to ever convey what is felt in my

heart. *Forever* seems to be the only word fitting of the timelessness we share, and of the *we* I've come to know and cherish. It's as if we're continuing down a sacred path designed centuries ago, promising then, as we do now, never to forget.

Perhaps the finest gift he brings me is the ever-present reminder of why God put us here: to care, nurture, and protect one another; to share the wonder; to give more than we take; to take the leap of faith; to believe in the power of the human spirit; and to live each day with the knowledge that love is the ladder to the stars, the very path to heaven. The gift I hope to give him back is my devotion to sharing these truths with the world.

It's been weeks since sharing coffee on that city corner. Weeks since the tears flowed so easily. We only had a moment then, and, like feathers floating across an ethereal sky, moments are all we will ever have. But, oh, how golden are they.

This morning, as I rushed through my routine, a thought interrupted my chaos to reveal peace. In a whispered tone, so familiar to my soul, I heard his voice in the wind. "I'm carrying you in my pocket . . . encouraging every footstep . . . so close in spirit . . . remember, it has no end."

Caressing the comfort, I realized my breathing had changed. I gazed at the wonder of the sky, knowing deep in my heart that a greater force, far above the windy city, arranged this gift in our lives. Unbroken is this understanding. Unbroken is this shared language of the soul. This is the definition of grace. This is forever friendship.

And yes, *He* planned it this way.

Time and distance

have no meaning.

Love is the beauty

we take with us

wherever we go.

Dear Heart

by Lisa Weedn

$\mathcal{I}$ saw it in his eyes. Eyes that had witnessed far more of life than most ever do. I felt it in his hands, trembling now from age. The seasons of time had not left him untouched.

Saul was in his eighties. Once a tall, lanky man in his youth, he now walked with the crook of an old oak tree. Bent, curved, but rich with wisdom and dimension was he. Saul was my neighbor, my friend. A man whom I adored.

It was fall when we first met. The turn of the leaves had just begun, as much as they do here in California. Being a native, I had grown to appreciate the subtleties. He stood at my door, introduced himself with a rhyme and a bowl of persimmons. Then, with a warm and brilliant laugh, he extended his hand. From that moment on, we've never let go.

He and his wife, Esther, a woman he gazed upon with the eyes of a young boy deeply in love, lived just across the street from me. She was a round, colorful woman, with long wisps of thick white hair she wore

43

tangled atop her head in an emerald-encrusted hair pin. Esther's body was twisted by arthritis, but she still owned a certain air of passion that made her compelling and strikingly beautiful. Age can never take away the mark of being loved.

She'd often tell the story of when Saul gave her the hair pin. "It was his grandmother's. He gave it to me wrapped in a poem on the day he asked me to marry him. The happiest day of my life," she'd say with pride, her eyes twinkling with girlhood charm. "I was just a young thing, with coal black hair and bright eyes. My mother wanted me to marry Evan, the doctor, but he was such a bore. Saul was from the other side of town. He was working odd jobs to pay his way through school. Not a dime to his name, but he was the only man who ever made me feel alive and beautiful. All things were possible when Saul held my hand. When your heart feels this way, my dear, there is only one path to take. Happiest day of my life, I tell you." In the nine months I knew them, I came to know this story well, but never tired of hearing it. Saul would sit across from her, reach for her hand, and re-live the moment with each telling. Theirs was a love story that had lasted over sixty years, and it was still in full bloom.

Saul and Esther invited me over almost daily. I was in my twenties back then and time allowed me the luxury. It became our treasured afternoon ritual.

They'd serve me fresh juice from their fruit trees, often some unique mixture Saul would concoct. "Taste the bitter and sweet," he'd say. "The bitter is life, the sweet is the love that makes it worth living." Saul never said anything that didn't move me. I loved him for the way his mind wove poetry into the fabric of life.

They never could have children, so in a way Saul and Esther took me in as their own. They'd often thank me for the time I gave, but I knew it was I who was blessed. They taught me more about love than any other couple I've ever met. They're still teaching me.

We'd sit in their backyard and take our turn sharing stories. Esther was a sculptress, and when her hands permitted, she'd still work the clay with a master's vision. Their garden was lush, filled with Saul's fruit trees, the iris patch he adored, and Esther's sculptures were everywhere. On tree stumps and benches, on boxes and crates, Saul proudly displayed her work, every one the image of a child. "My dear heart, she's such a talent. She could've been famous. But instead she made us a family of clay. Luckiest man alive, I am, luckiest in the world," he'd say, then bend down and kiss her clay-covered hand.

When Saul wasn't attending to her every need, bringing Esther water to douse the drying clay she struggled to form, or scurrying about making sure she took her medication at the appropriate hour, he'd read me his poetry. Witty, intelligent, and romantic was he. I was in awe of his grasp of humanity, of love, and of the stream of lucid thought that belied his years. The first poem he ever read to me was the very one he used to propose to Esther. Although written by a young Saul, innocent and deeply in love, it was as true to life today as it was back then.

```
Esther, Dear Heart

In the mist of a dream
You come to me
Is this earth or heaven
Or the passage in between
Tell me with your eyes
That forever you'll be mine
Share my earth and heaven
Beyond the end of time
In the mist of a dream
And all the passages in between

Your Saul
October 10, 1925
```

Saul rarely left the house, save for on Saturdays when he attended his poetry group. This was the day he hired a nurse to come be with Esther, for he never left her alone. The retreat gave him something to look forward to and provided him storytelling material for Esther and me in the week ahead. He'd muse over the wrinkled crowd of ten who joined him. Their offerings made him sad at times, and he'd say in a hushed tone, "So much of life to tell, when you're old — so much lost, so much found. Sad to think no one listens but your own kind. Tell your tale while you can, child. Sing it to the world. And one day, maybe you can tell mine. I used to be a lawyer in Brooklyn. Now I'm a romantic old poet who picks persimmons. You think you can make a story of that?" He'd chuckle, then add, "If you do, don't forget my dear heart Esther. No story of mine can ever be complete without her in it. She's my life, my reason for being here. Stay true to your heart and one day you shall know the same."

Saul took ill before summer arrived, and I watched the ambulance carry him away. I drove Esther to the hospital and stayed until I knew it was time for them to be alone. Saul was fading, we all knew it, and I wanted their ending to be as close as their beginning. Just the two of them, rapt in the waltz. Before I left, I said my goodbyes in private thought, fighting back the tears. I took his hand and stroked his cheek, etching the memory in my heart. He looked up at me and in a faint voice said, "Taste the bitter and sweet, child. And don't forget to pick the persimmons." He left us that very night, and within days, Esther, too, was gone. They departed this world together, a promise I'm sure they made to one another. As it was meant to be.

Their nephew flew in from the East. Knowing little of his aunt and uncle, I was pleased when he asked me my thoughts about their memorial service. I had only three wishes to offer: fill the room with irises from Saul's garden; place Esther's favorite sculptures, her *children*, near the podium; and lay Esther to rest wearing her beloved hair pin. He obliged, and somehow I felt a certain peace. It was my small gift to two souls who taught me the meaning of forever love.

Scores of people attended their service. Little did Saul and Esther know the many lives they had touched. I felt my heart saying, "Look, Saul, they were listening!" Ten writers stood to read poems written for Saul. How proud he would have been to hear their praise, as creations from Esther's own hands looked on. Finally, I stood, and shared the poem Saul had read to me some nine months before, and to Esther over sixty years ago. The beginning of their dream on earth seemed a fitting beginning to their next passage.

In the mist of a dream
You come to me
Is this earth or heaven
Or the passage in between . . .

*B*elieve in

your H E A R T

that something

wonderful is

about to **happen**.

Unexpected Miracles

In every moment
of time, as in every
footprint in the sand,
there lies hope, and
strength, and wisdom.

A Morning Walk

by Lisa Weedn

We awoke with the dawn, my daughter and I. The restless woman within me was thankful for my daughter's bright spirit and her gentle voice. Her smile, her sheer beauty gave me strength and focus.

"Let's go, Mama," I heard her say. "Let's explore the world. It's just you and me today."

I threw on torn jeans, an ancient white tee and a baseball cap, my favorite. She, too, wore a cap much like my own, her golden hair spilling out like shimmering glass. We gathered muffins, crusts of bread for the seagulls, and the ripest oranges we could find. We set out on our journey, kicked off our shoes within moments, and felt the cold sand beneath our toes. We dug in deeply, feeling the smooth and rocky texture of the earth's wonder.

We talked of life, this infant child and I. Already more than mother and daughter, ancient friends we had become. Her wisdom belied her youthful form. The wonder she shared daily offered me my greatest teachings. Her ever-present awareness of life's beauty was something she owned more clearly than I, it

53

seemed. She left me in awe. She still does.

"What color is heaven, Mama? How high is the sky? Does God sit on a porch as he watches our footsteps? Tell me about love."

I listened, as my heart filled. The tears I could not contain. The answers I could not speak. Only the strong grasp of my hand told her what she needed to know.

She smiled and ran before me, exploring the waves as they splashed upon her legs. Her laughter, the song I cherish most. I watched her with newfound eyes. She was me, though in a smaller form. She was more, dancing with dreams, so open and free, holding all the world's tomorrows in her tiny, precious hands.

Both of us in the water now, drenched up to our knees. The air still cold, the sun hiding behind the grayness of the sky. The fresh beginning of the day was ours to behold. We felt it, we drank it up, while others slept warm in their beds, missing this glory.

Shivering a bit, we welcomed a break in the clouds and rested against a rock. Spreading out a piece of cloth, we designed a breakfast picnic before us. The seagulls rounded, scores of them, hungry for attention. The crumbs we threw, they devoured. Their sounds, my daughter imitated. More laughter. All of us feeding on this moment. Life's nourishment.

We were alone on the beach, at least we thought we were, until the sound of footsteps approached. A homeless woman, cold, hungry, and not much older than myself, caught our eye. Trying to force a smile, she walked before us, too ashamed to look up.

Before I could speak, my daughter cried out. "Would you like a muffin? We've got lots to share." The woman looked up in disbelief. I said not a word. This was a moment between them. I watched. I listened. The woman's sundried skin summoned a deeper smile. She turned and moved toward us. Beneath the pain, her eyes were kind.

"That would be nice, if you have any to spare," she replied in a whisper.

"Oh yeah, of course we do," my daughter said. "Come sit. We're safe. Want a blanket? What's your name? Do you like oranges?"

Now the three of us, sitting cross-legged on the sand. Surrounded by seagulls devouring crumbs. Squawking, squealing, were they. Smiling, were we. Then a moment of silence, as we shared an early thanksgiving.

We exchanged names, though not much more. The pain of truth was too difficult to reveal. We did not ask. Instead we shared a quiet comfort, void of fear or judgment. Strangers were we, though not really.

I don't know how long we sat there, but the moments were rich and full. Somehow they completed the picture of life's intention and answered the questions I had been searching for. The morning had brought to each of us a gift, and my daughter and the stranger were entwined in the knowing, the unspoken understanding of it all.

The purpose of our meetings in life is not important — the magic is, the sharing, the unified care, kindness, and silent strength we offer one another. The unconditional acceptance that we are all the same inside. No matter who we are or what path we are following, we are all connected to one another in the mystery, the pain, and the beauty of life.

My daughter hugged her before she walked away, as did I, and her scent I will not forget. Nor will I ever lose the vision of her feet wearing my shoes — the only thing she would accept from me, save for the unspoken. My daughter invited her back, though I doubt we will ever see her again, but with us she will always remain. I pray she'll remember us, too.

Heading back for home now, my daughter looked up at me with a knowing smile. "I know the color of heaven, Mama. It is the color of your eyes. And love? It's what we just felt."

Life's promises don't always come true, but mornings still come, and birds still sing in the trees.

Tree of Heaven

by Flavia Weedn

It was late afternoon, and I was eight years old. Walking across the vacant lot near our house, I was looking for wild flowers and dreaming that we lived somewhere else — anywhere else. To me, everything in this neighborhood was old and forgotten. Sometimes it made me feel the same way.

While stepping over the railroad tracks, I noticed this skinny, little whisper of a tree with its long leaves. It was growing among others like it, in the dirty dust beside the tracks. The older trees around it were much taller, with large oval-shaped leaves that curved downward along each branch. From a distance, each group of branches looked like open umbrellas trying to protect whatever was growing under them.

But this little tree was young, frail-looking, and growing too close to the tracks. I was afraid the next train would destroy it, so I brought it home. Mama was used to me rescuing living things, but this was the first time I had ever brought home a tree. She just smiled, re-planted it beside our back porch steps, and told me it was called a *Tree of Heaven*. She knew all about it because one had grown near her house when she was a little girl.

Other trees grew in our yard, but this one was different. For some reason, its very presence at our back door seemed significant to me. Perhaps it was because I felt it belonged there, although I didn't know why. The next day, the tree was taller. It grew so quickly that many times at night after dinner, my younger brother, Willie, and I would sit on the back porch and watch it for hours just to see if we could see it grow.

One such night Mama joined us, and the three of us sat there quietly. I didn't see it growing, but I did see how beautiful the young tree looked in the moonlight, even beside those old porch steps. After a while, Mama told us everything she knew about this very unusual kind of tree.

We learned from her that the tree grows near old buildings and houses that have been boarded-up and deserted or beside railroad tracks, vacant lots, and in junkyards. It finds its way up through cellar gratings, out of holes in alleys; under old broken fences, and near piles of rubbish. It grows lush and green, strong and tall, all the while needing very little sun, water or earth. "If you look at the tree with your heart and really see it," Mama said, "it seems as though it's determined to touch the sky."

Before she said good-night, she told us she had always believed that God had given the tree its name because He wanted children to learn from it. God planted it in places where children could discover it, and see that no matter where they lived, they could make their dreams reach for the sky. Just like this tree.

Willie and I exchanged long thoughts about our *Tree of Heaven*. Why it was I happened to find it beside those railroad tracks and wanted to bring it home that day — and why it seemed different than any other tree we'd ever seen.

We decided I didn't just happen upon that little tree, there was a reason I needed to find it that afternoon. The tree was there to show me that, to God, there are no forgotten neighborhoods or children just people like me who sometimes need to be reminded that each person matters.

Willie and I had learned one thing more: why a skinny, little tree, the one Mama called the *Tree of Heaven*, was the only tree that could grow through cement. God had shown it how to believe in hope.

From that moment on, I knew He had not forgotten me. God was all around me — in the moon and stars and the mornings and the nights. He was in the hearts and hopes of all children everywhere, whenever they wished and dreamed and prayed. It makes no difference who or where we are, God believes in us and wants us to believe in ourselves.

Together we reasoned that our tree must be one of His small miracles, if not on earth, then at least in our neighborhood. I closed my eyes and, before I went to sleep, said my prayers and thanked God for sending us this tree. I knew this had been one of the most beautiful nights of my life; a night I would never forget. The mere thought that there was a miracle growing in our backyard made my whole body fill with hope and pure happiness.

Hope is one of the connections between heaven and earth. It is a beautiful, golden cord woven of faith and believing. And should times come to make us doubt its existence, something beautiful will always happen to remind us that it is never lost. Hope may become hidden or covered up a bit, but it never leaves us. It is there all the time, somewhere in the heart.

Each of us is born with hope, and if we believe in it and hold it close, it will last forever. Maybe even longer.

Change is a courageous dance whose delicate steps are made of strength and dreams, for within each of us are wings yearning to fly.

Dancing Wings

by Flavia Weedn

Trees surround our old Spanish house, the most majestic being a large California Redwood, several hundred years old. Standing more than sixty feet tall, it watches over us, and protects us while its wide, full branches spread outward like giant wings. They offer shelter to the butterflies that frequent our yard and to a variety of birds, from sparrows to large black crows. From the wooden swing that hangs from one of its lower branches, I can watch the smaller birds dart from limb to limb, and listen to the crows as they dance on the topmost branches.

When my granddaughter, Sylvie, was four years old, she began joining me on Saturday mornings. We created a routine in which we first would sit quietly together in the swing and breathe in the fragrance of this beautiful old tree. Suddenly, as though she heard music, she would take my hand and we would dance under the low branches. The moment always came when she would let go and dance alone with arms outstretched.

With her imaginary wings, she gracefully swayed between the sunlight and shadows. I prayed she would never let the world take from her the wonder I saw in her face.

Reaching for my hand again, the dance became a nature walk of discovery beneath the tree. Sylvie would lead the way under the branches where we'd gather pine cones and look for doodlebugs and butterflies. I listened closely while she carefully described the beautiful, tiny world of elves and fairies that she knew lived under the toadstools near the large sculpted roots of the tree. She told me that if I looked closely enough and believed, I might be able to see them, too. She also reminded me that they really were for children to see, that's why grown-up people usually couldn't see them.

Near the tree there is a covered patio, with two sides attached to the house. The third side is a half-wall, above which are large glass windowpanes overlooking the rose garden. The remaining side is entirely open, except for an old wooden gate that leads back to the tree. Once Sylvie mastered the latch on this gate, she would guide me from the tree up the path to the garden, then to the steps where she proudly unlatched the gate. This she did each time with great pride, before we would step onto the patio.

Recently, while we were having a snack on this

patio, Sylvie noticed a small butterfly. He kept darting repeatedly into the same glass windowpane directly above the patio wall. Again and again he would hit the glass in the same spot. I concluded the day was so bright and clear, the glass must have looked invisible to the butterfly, causing him to make these futile attempts to fly through it. He continually tried to reach the light and touch the roses on the other side. I could see that the windowpane ended just to the left of the butterfly into the open air. If he had flown just two or three inches in a slightly different direction, he would have been beyond the window and completely free to fly anywhere.

As we watched the butterfly's struggle, Sylvie, half thinking out loud, asked me in a tender, little voice why the butterfly didn't just fly around the glass instead of trying to fly through it in the same place, over and over again. "He's so close to the outside," she said, "and he doesn't even know it." She followed with, "Come, Mimi, we have to show him how." Ever so carefully, and despite the rapid fluttering of his wings, we were able to carefully guide him that short distance until the butterfly was away from the glass and able to fly toward the garden.

As we continued our walk, I realized how easy it is for us, as people, to fall into the same kind of trap as that butterfly. When we are faced with anything from a dilemma to a heartache, we usually try to get through it by using a method that has worked for us before. If we keep trying and trying and this method doesn't help, we eventually lose hope and give up. But that's not the solution.

Life doesn't always give us someone to lead the way or show us how, as it did for the butterfly. Obstacles will always come before us, and the clearer and more defined they seem, the easier it is for us to think we can get through them the same way we have before. When this doesn't work, we need to allow our minds and hearts to look at the situation from a different point of view. From a different perspective, we can find the strength to become unafraid to try again. Once we see we can reach the light from a new direction, we find our way into the garden.

I believe we are given problems so that we can learn how to overcome them, and that we grow from the process of that experience. But it is how we meet the challenge, and what we've learned and become after we've worked our way through that matters most. There is where the gifts are found.

Sylvie is older now, and we continue to take walks and I continue to listen to her as she tells me about the elves and fairies and the pure beauty she finds in nature. I know that someday when she's older, she'll touch upon the memory of that butterfly. She'll realize

that in those few moments on that patio, she had discovered there was another gift in addition to beauty and imagination in nature; there was knowledge.

And when the day comes and it's time for her to spread her real wings and dance, I am certain her dance will be guided by what she's learned from nature, and she will follow her heart wherever it tells her to go.

We are

each a part

of one another.

Care is

the *golden thread*

that connects

us all.

Gifts

of

Grace

*The understanding
heart builds a stage,
where a gathering of
dreams can dance.*

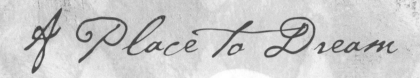

A Place To Dream

by Flavia Weedn

My father's friends were unique. Most were casual friends, those he'd met at a bar, sat next to on a bus, or worked with briefly on one of his overseas jobs. They never stayed in his life very long, they kept moving on, looking for something that most could never find. They were the lonely ones, often the companionless, those the world seemed to have forgotten.

There was a period in the early 1950's when some of his friends, uninvited, would knock at our door around dinner time on Sunday afternoons. My dad never introduced them because he'd forgotten most of their names. After a few minutes he became bored. He'd grab some food, a good cigar, then leave the room, and go to bed. Without saying goodnight, he had a way of just slowly disappearing. He was like that.

My mother was filled with kindness and she gave it even to strangers. When she did this, I always thought this was her way of feeling she was paying back for some of the joy she found in living.

"They're lonely," she would reason to my brother and me in her Southern way. "It's Sunday and they have no place to go. It's just dinner, and there's enough food to go around. Now, be nice."

I'm not sure we ever knew where my dad met his friend, Pierre. What we did know was that Pierre and his girlfriend, Eunice, found their way to our house almost every Sunday for two months. They never called first, they just came. They came to talk about Eunice, while we listened.

Pierre was in his late fifties, short, slight, and rather dapper, with a thin, narrow mustache. He was nice enough looking, but a man one would pass on the street and not notice. He wore pin-striped pleated pants and a felt hat. I remember wondering if he could have been an old friend of my dad's from Dallas, because men from Texas always wore hats then. But I never asked.

Eunice was different. A woman one would definitely remember. She was also short, but rather round, big bosomed and older than Pierre. The color of her fluffy hair varied from an orange red to a golden red. Her make-up also varied, as though she tried new color combinations every Sunday. Her hands were pale, unmarked, with manicured nails so long, I wondered how she buttoned and unbuttoned anything.

She described herself as an actress and the mother of a famous athlete. The clothes she wore were a dressy cocktail style, with a look that suggested they were

expensive once, but a long time ago.

Inside Pierre's dark green Plymouth, there appeared to be everything they owned. Her things, arranged with care, filled the front and back seats of the car, leaving just enough room for each of them to sit. One Sunday, Pierre opened the trunk to show my brother and me his golf clubs, revealing his belongings stacked over, under, and around his clubs.

I had wondered earlier if they lived in his car, but after seeing how full its interior, I knew that notion would have been physically impossible. Whenever I asked, Eunice always said they were moving, or just getting settled in their new place. Pierre simply said they had been together for twelve years and that she was from Hollywood.

On Sundays they always sat in the center of the couch, which became their stage. My mother, when she wasn't cooking, sat in a chair opposite them, my little brother and I on the floor. Eunice would mention she had just received a romantic script for her perusal. She followed with stories about producers fighting over her, and how each wanted her exclusively. The stories wandered on and on, and somewhere within the Sundays that followed, the Hollywood producers got lost and became Broadway producers.

After every dinner, Pierre would unfold a napkin and place it on the arm of the couch. From a pocket, he'd bring out several chocolates, and place them upon the napkin. At first, my little brother and I were fascinated, thinking he was going to perform a magic trick of some kind, but we were wrong.

Eunice would delicately select one chocolate at a time, eating slowly as she ended her final story for the evening. My brother and I laughed to ourselves, and sometimes thought watching this part of their show was better than a movie. We were their audience, but knew early on that a script never existed. It was simply an opening into this actress role she chose to play, for some reason, in our living room.

The Sundays wore on. Eunice would mention more scripts, and films she was going to make. By then, meetings in famous Hollywood restaurants had begun to float in and out of her stories, while Pierre continued to serve her chocolates.

One chilly Sunday, she told us she would have worn her fur coat, but it was in storage. She said she'd wear it the next Sunday, to see how my mother liked it, because she was leaving it to her in her will. Eunice said she knew about colors, and thought it would go nicely with my mom's complexion and dark hair.

Next Sunday came and so did Eunice and Pierre, but no sight or word of a fur. She spoke of the recent feats of her supposedly famous son, which were word for word, quite coincidentally, as they appeared that

morning in the newspaper. Before they left, there was a new story of her previous marriage to some movie star icon. The saga seemed endless.

But it wasn't, for that was the last Sunday we spent with them. Pierre called my mother, said it was time for them to move on, that they were leaving California. He knew that she knew the stories Eunice had been telling us were her fantasies, and deeply thanked Mama for her kindness and patience.

When Eunice was young, he said, it was true, she had lived in Hollywood. She'd dreamed all those years of being in the movies, but it never happened. As her youth faded, she became more and more alone. When she found it too difficult to live her life as it was, she invented a new one. Then she met Pierre. To him she was still young and beautiful, because he loved her as she was. Eunice loved him because he was the only one who listened.

To my mother, her time with them had never been about kindness or patience. It was about understanding. I was blessed with a mother who knew that the human heart needs a place to dream, and for awhile, we were that place for Eunice. My mother, in her wisdom, had understood this from the beginning.

My six-year-old granddaughter also knows this. I was reminded of it recently when I asked why she always played in my closet when she pretended, and

77

she answered, "Mimi, don't you understand? When I'm at your house, I have to have a place to be a princess, and this closet is my place." I understood.

❧

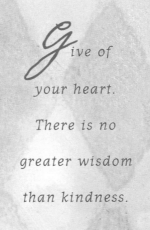

*G*ive of
your heart.
There is no
greater wisdom
than kindness.

A Friend Next Door

by Flavia Weedn

She lived next door to us, and she was old like her house. No one knew her first name, although she'd lived there forever. Mama understood that she was Mrs. Morgan, and said we should call her that. But my brother and I didn't call her anything, we just stayed away. Like all the other kids on the block, we were afraid of her. She was mean, like a witch.

Anytime a ball would accidentally go into her yard, she took it. She yelled at us whenever we rode our bikes down the alley behind her house. Once we found a hungry stray cat, and Willie and I tried to catch it before it ran toward her house. We never saw it again, and we thought she killed it to keep it away from the green apple tree in her yard. She rarely came out of her house, except when she watered that prized tree, and even then she spoke to no one.

Willie and I sat on the curb every Saturday morning and waited for the bakery truck. The driver would blow his whistle, stop the truck in front of our house and pull out the shelves filled with freshly baked pastries. That wonderful aroma floated around

81

us like a cloud. We would already be eating before everyone else on our street gathered around and tried samples of cream puffs and chocolate eclairs. Everyone, except Mrs. Morgan. She was the only one whose door remained closed.

On Halloween night, she put up no decorations, kept the lights out, and never came to the door. At Christmastime, there was only silence and darkness coming from her house. It was the first time I realized I was feeling a little sorry for Mrs. Morgan.

Sometimes at night, from our bedroom window we could see clearly into the curtain-less window of her kitchen. We never saw her there, but about once a week we still continued to look, rationalizing it was only to see if she were still alive. In reality, we were young and curious about this strange woman. She was the neighborhood mystery, and we wanted to know why. Although my brother and I didn't think there was anything really wrong with looking into her window, we decided not to tell Mama. But one night Mama saw us.

With wisdom instead of anger, she proceeded to teach her children a lesson about life, and quietly led us into the kitchen. We sat motionless and watched while she lit the oven and rolled out cookie dough. She placed the baked cookies onto a plate, covered it with waxed paper, and tied a purple ribbon around it. She told us the cookies weren't for us, and to go to bed. I

closed my eyes, and in the darkness my thoughts were clear. I knew who the cookies were for.

Very early the next day, with Mama directing us, we climbed under the fence. Putting the cookies on her back porch, we knocked on Mrs. Morgan's door, then ran home. Mid-morning we heard the sound of water running. There she stood in her yard, watering her apple tree. The brass hose nozzle shimmered in her hands from the sunlight through the clouds, and for a moment there was a slight hint of a smile on her face. Mama said the lesson had begun.

Late that afternoon, Mama stood on a stepladder to reach a quilt on the top shelf of the closet. Handing it down to me, she said it was for Mrs. Morgan. Her enclosed note said that we didn't need this quilt and thought perhaps she might, now that it was turning cold. Mama signed it with Willie's and my name. I wondered how Mrs. Morgan would know who we were, but Mama said she'd know. We wrapped the quilt in tissue paper, folded it into a large grocery bag and, as soon as it was dark, put the bag on her porch. We peeked through the fence and, within a few moments, it was gone.

For the next two days, we saw and heard nothing from Mrs. Morgan. On the night of the second day, there was a knock at our back door and the sound of feet scurrying. Mama opened the door to find a pie still warm from the oven. We knew from the distinctive smell of green apples exactly who had put it there. With it was a note of thanks addressed to Willie and me. Mrs. Morgan had written in pencil, and signed it: — *from your friend, Alma.*

Mrs. Morgan saw us catch a glimpse of her under her porch light just before she went back inside her house. She held a cat in her arms. It was the stray Willie and I had tried to catch, only now a purple ribbon was tied around its neck. Mrs. Morgan smiled, pointed to the cat, and said, "Her name is Friend, and you both can come over and play with her anytime you like!"

There are those like Mrs. Morgan living in many of our neighborhoods today. The woman often lives alone and keeps to herself. If you happen to see her, she's wrapped in a faded apron, sweeping her porch or sidewalk more often than need be. If she's going to church, she'll be wearing a hat she's had for years, and soft white gloves — and the color of her handbag will match the scarf she wears to hide the wrinkles on her neck. No matter which direction she's going, she'll be walking with her head down as though she's following an invisible path. The man will be wearing suspenders and usually a sweater, even though it's not cold. He'll need a shave, and rarely be without his hat. If he's sitting on a bench at the corner, he'll have a newspaper under his arm and the exact change for the

bus in his hand. He or she may live just down the street from you; they'll be the ones who water their yard and groom their roses most every day, waiting for someone, anyone, to say hello.

Life is busier and more demanding now than when I was a child. We have less time to notice people like Mrs. Morgan, yet in their lives they have more time than anything else. If we put forth the effort to really see them, we can discover a real and quiet beauty and be deeply touched, for they have simple and wise stories to tell. A simple act of kindness could change their lives, and maybe ours, for when we give of our hearts we are giving a most blessed gift to ourselves.

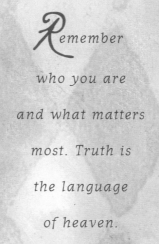

*Remember
who you are
and what matters
most. Truth is
the language
of heaven.*

Amazing Grace

by Lisa Weedn

$\mathcal{I}$nspiration. Peace. Truth. Fulfillment. We all share in the quest. We all know the intimate yearning. Deep inside we are all spiritual beings, in spite of the many different costumes we wear. But the alarm goes off, and the bills need to be paid, and a child needs soothing, and, alas, the hourglass spills its sand faster than we can dance.

How easy it is to lose our footing, for the very act of living requires so much of us. Still, in the sacred silence of our minds, we attempt to weave together a golden thread of hope and conviction that keeps us balanced, in motion, passionately driven. Some of us find it in our work, in the nurturing of our family, in our faith, or in our art. Whatever it is that rings the bell within us, we must stay attentive to the sound and keep our eyes open to the vision. For if we look, as the prophets have said, we shall find. Even within the chaos.

It was early morning and I sat in an old wooden chair in our living room. My daughter sat cross-legged at my feet. As I brushed her long silken hair, she hummed her own rendition of *Amazing Grace*, and

I knew her thoughts were far away from this room. Mine, however, were secretly racing with the clock; plotting hour by hour the tasks that lay in wait. I felt the rush of a breeze and spied the kiss of sunlight on her face, streaming in through the open window, catching the purity of her eyes. My thoughts had been rushed, hers were oblivious to time, but in that instant I felt the light reach me. It was as if I were being called to remember how precious the moments are, how fleeting the years can be, and how easy it can be to forget.

I began harmonizing with her, secretly drifting to my own private place of reflection, until she jumped up and said, "Ok, let's go now. Hurry, Mama, we can't be late." Ah, that clock again. With a sigh, I rose to my feet, and together we gathered our tools for the day. Hers: a backpack, homework, a hastily made lunch, and a favorite book to share. Mine: manuscripts, unfinished sketches and a spare set of spectacles for tired eyes which were destined to give out by day's end. Then off we went, thrusting ourselves back into the routine of the race.

By late morning I was already donning my specs, my shoulders ached and I was overwhelmed by deadlines. Little signs were surfacing, small reminders everywhere, still I hadn't yet acknowledged what was happening. I was juggling plates, far too many of them, and it was only a matter of time before they

would all come crashing to the floor.

"Hurry, there's not much time!" was the ever-present voice I heard in my mind. "Sorry, baby, Mama's got to work," was the line my daughter had to hear too often. "No, I can't. Maybe next month," was the response I gave to the few patient friends who loved me enough to remain interested. I was losing my balance. I was so caught up in the process of my passion that I had forgotten the purpose. Time, precious time, had become my enemy. I needed a wake-up call.

That call came just after lunch. A tiny voice said "I skinned my knee real bad, Mama. It hurts. Can you pick me up early? Please?" My decision was easy. Although weary, I dropped my work and headed toward my daughter's school.

I drove in silence, my mind attempting to sort out the myriad of questions I was asking myself. Then I remembered a dear friend's wisdom. In order to see clearly, he once told me, sometimes we have to step out of the circle. When life gets hard, take a pause. Step out. Look inside. Therein you'll find the answer.

My daughter was waiting for me when I arrived. Her excitement over the opportunity to leave school early, and steal an afternoon with me, made her injury bearable. With a bandaged knee and a paint-stained dress, she met me with a smile. Hungry arms wrapped themselves around me, as she whispered in my ear, "I love you so, Mama."

Just the vision of her, the touch of her small hand, the music of her voice moved me to a higher place. I gazed at her for an extended moment, and felt the tears slip down my cheek. She said not a word, just sidled up beside me in the car and entwined her fingers in mine. She squeezed tightly. So did I.

We agreed this might be a good time for ice cream, and drove to a local drug store. A man with deeply compassionate eyes greeted us behind the counter. As he handed us our sugar cones, he slipped me a business card which read: *Details for Care*. I looked up at him, puzzled. He smiled back and explained. He was a full-time reverend, a part-time ice cream clerk, and three weekends a month he detailed cars to raise money to care for homeless families. On the fourth weekend he fed them.

"We always need a hand, if you can find the time," he said, and I looked on the back of the card to find an address and a date — the very date I recognized as an important work deadline. I shrugged, and began to offer my regrets. But something made me pause. I looked over at my daughter, her eyes speaking volumes, breathlessly awaiting my answer. Step out of the circle, I heard my inner voice say. Then I began again, "Of course, Reverend, we'll be there."

"Bless you," he said in response.

"No. Bless you," I smiled in return.

My daughter's face beamed, and together we stepped into the light. Like the hint of breeze through the morning window, the message was clear. It was an honor to be alive and healthy and able. This life was a privilege, and time was not an enemy, it was a precious gift. I must give thanks for the blessing and never, ever forget to share the miracle.

For the first time in months I felt a sense of balance return. The weight of my deadlines, my illusionary race with time, my tired and burdened reality were each a result of my blindness, not my vision. I didn't need to reduce the tasks at hand. I didn't need to pour more sand into the hourglass. All I needed was to remember what mattered most. Love was the purpose behind everything. Love for my daughter, my family. Love for humanity. Love for God. This was the golden thread of my passion, the source of my peace and my strength — the very conviction of my soul. This is what made the impossible possible. I silently offered a prayer.

My daughter and I climbed into the car. And with ice cream smiles, we began harmonizing our private rendition of *Amazing Grace*.

To the Reader

Our time on earth is made up of moments, each one sacred. We weave together precious strands of time to create the fabric of our living. It is a miraculous journey we all share, this tapestry of human experience, for it is rich with blessed offerings and the wonder of God's subtlety and grace.

From sunrise to starry night, life's miracles are shown to us, be they in the beauty of a harvest moon or in the magic of an embrace. The sight of a child's tender smile, the act of giving back more than we take, the power of love and the comforting blanket of friendship all rekindle the light of faith in our hearts and serve to remind us what is most important.

Being gratefully aware of it all is the silken thread linking us to the finest miracle — the very privilege of being alive. Let us never forget, this journey is far too brief and fragile to let moments go by without acknowledging the wondrous gift we have been given.

In writing this book, we were graced with the divine opportunity of sharing with you treasures we have saved within our souls. We hope that you have felt a kindred understanding, a warm touch of faith, and a deeper reverence for all the treasures you hold dear. Most of all, we hope that you will be moved to give abundant thanks for your own tapestry of life, and that in doing so you will discover the fabric you have woven is more beautiful than you ever dared to dream.

In gratitude,

Flavia and Lisa Weedn

Flavia

Lisa and her daughter Sylvie

Flavia Weedn is one of America's leading contemporary inspirational writers and illustrators. Offering hope for the human spirit, Flavia portrays the basic excitement, simplicity and beauty she sees in the ordinary things of life. Her work has touched the lives of millions for over three decades.

Lisa Weedn, Flavia's daughter and co-author, shares her mother's philosophy and passion. For over fifteen years, Lisa's writings have been a quiet messenger of the fundamental truth that age has no barrier on feelings of the human heart.

Their collaborative work, which celebrates life and embraces meaningful core values, can be found in numerous books, collections of fine stationery goods, giftware, and lifestyle products distributed worldwide.

Flavia and Lisa live in Santa Barbara, California.